A *Dazzle* *of* Hummingbirds

THE COLORFUL LIFE OF A TINY SCRAPPER

BY BRUCE BERGER

LONDON TOWN PRESS

The London Town *Wild Life* Series
Series Editor
Vicki León

A Dazzle of Hummingbirds
Photographers
John Chellmans; Kay Comstock; Michael Fogden; Clayton Fogle;
Jeff Foott; John Gerlach; François Gohier; Marcia Griffen;
Richard Hansen; Noah Hawthorne; Stephen Krasemann;
Wayne Lankinen; George Lepp; Pat O'Hara; L.L.T. Rhodes;
Doug Wechsler

London Town Press
P.O. Box 585
Montrose, California 91021
www.LondonTownPress.com

Book design by Christy Hale
10   9   8   7   6   5   4   3   2   1

Printed in Singapore

Distributed by Publishers Group West

Publisher's Cataloging-in-Publication Data
Berger, Bruce.
A dazzle of hummingbirds : the colorful life of a tiny scrapper
/ Bruce Berger.—2nd ed.
p.   cm. — (London Town wild life series)
Originally published: San Luis Obispo, CA : Blake Books
©1993
Summary: An introduction to the life cycle, migratory patterns
and behavior of various species of hummingbirds, illustrated
with vivid photographs.
Includes bibliographic references and index.
ISBN 0-9666490-7-9
1. Hummingbirds—Juvenile literature. [1. Hummingbirds.]
I. Title. II. Series.
QL696.A558 B47 2005
598.764—dc22
2004117672

FRONT COVER: A broad-billed hummer uses its bright red beak
to find nectar and insects in a pink thistle.

TITLE PAGE: A female of the Anna's hummingbird species
seems to hang in space as she hovers, sipping from a
fuchsia or two.

HABITAT SHOWCASE: A garden (pp. 6-7); alpine meadow
(pp. 12-13); cloud forest (pp. 26-27); or desert (pp. 38-39)
provide different hummingbird species with different sources
of nectar and shelter.

BACK COVER: A ruby-throated hummer perches on a berry
branch, madly flashing his colors at a possible mate—or
a rival.

Contents

Superlative bird in a small package

Zing! A tiny thing with wings zooms, it zings, it circles our heads and scolds us with buzzes, clicks, and high-pitched squawks. Who is this little scrapper? The hummingbird, of course—one of the best loved creatures to add excitement and color to a garden or a park.

It's not much at carrying a tune. But the hummer can produce a ringing, zinging sound with its wings, as it flies forwards, backwards, up, down, sideways—or hovers in sheer space.

When the New World was first settled by Europeans in the 1600s, the colonists gaped in amazement at this bird, smaller than any known in Europe. New Englander William Wood wrote: "The humbird is one of the wonders of the Countrey…not bigger than a Hornet….as glorious as the Rainebow…."

He was describing the ruby-throated hummer, the only species to live east of the Mississippi River. There are over 340 species of hummingbirds or Trochilidae, the second largest family of birds in the Western Hemisphere.

These little busybodies range across North and South America, from icy Alaska south to the tip of Argentina. In between, they inhabit tropical rainforests and mountain meadows, deserts, and mangrove swamps. Some species add their dazzle to many Carribbean islands in the Atlantic, while in the Pacific, a handful of hummers live on islands just west of South America.

Many species call the northern part of South America home, living in rainforests or cloud forests on either side of the equator. The country of Ecuador alone has 163 different kinds. But these small flyers also like heights. In the Andes Mountains, hummingbirds can be found up to the snow line.

This zest for heights shows up in the United States, too, where some 15 species nest in the mountainous west.

◄ Drinking deep from scarlet flowers on a salvia bush, a black-chinned hummer female beats her wings so fast, they are almost invisible.

Hummers thrive in many habitats. East of the Mississippi River, ruby-throateds such as this one favor forests, parks, and gardens. Out west, the same habitats attract Allen's and Anna's hummingbirds.

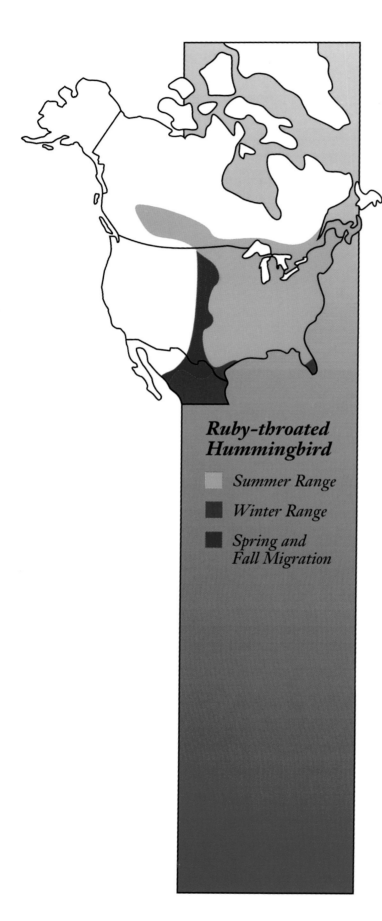

**Ruby-throated
Hummingbird**

⬜ *Summer Range*

⬛ *Winter Range*

⬛ *Spring and
Fall Migration*

Since many species make regular migrations, usually north and south, it's sometimes hard to say which is their true place of residence. In general, though, hummingbirds which have adapted to life in the rainforest tend to stay put. Most other hummingbirds follow the flowers. When the air gets nippy and the flowers are few, they migrate to warmer climates in the southwest United States, Mexico, Central America, and South America.

Hummers may have startled the European newcomers, but they were important and symbolic creatures to indigenous people like the Pima, the Hopi, and the Zuni of the southwestern United States, the Nazca people of Peru, the Taino Indians of the Caribbean, and the ancient Mayans and Aztecs of old Mexico.

The Pimas called them "rainbringers." The Taino named their best fighters "hummingbird warriors." The art of the Nazcas often focused on these birds. On the plains of Peru, you can still see a 300-foot-long hummingbird, carved into the earth by the Nazcas 1,500 years ago.

The Aztecs admired the hummingbird's feathers more than the living birds. Aztec nobles proudly wore cloaks that shimmered like rainbows, made from hundreds of tiny hummingbird skins.

Once Europeans discovered this bird, they treated it no better. For nearly 300 years, they conducted a brisk international trade in hummingbird skins to make brooches, hats, dustcatchers, and knicknacks for Victorian homes. In 1888 alone, over 400,000 skins were sold in London. Millions of birds died—all for

fashion and fad. A couple of species, now presumed to be extinct, are known only from their feathered bodies, sewn onto ladies' hats.

In the 20th century, laws were passed to restrict the trade in plants, animals, and birds, and a more enlightened era began. Human beings began to respect and protect wild creatures more. Today we can't imagine skinning a hummingbird.

These little creatures sparkle and sizzle like emeralds, rubies, and other gemstones. Bolting from flower to flower, they must

▲ A male rufous hovers, using its tail to give it extra lift. Hummers and helicopters have flight tricks in common: both can take off and land vertically, and even fly sideways or backwards. But a hummingbird moves its wings back and forth to fly; choppers fly by using blades that rotate in a circle.

have seemed like fragments of a waking dream to early explorers and settlers.

Color and beauty aren't the only things that make hummers superlative. It's hard to believe such mini-sized creatures can even be birds. The Cuban bee hummer—all two and one-quarter inches of it—weighs less than a penny, and is generally agreed to be the world's smallest bird. Even the world's largest hummingbird, an 8½-inch-long giant of the Andes, weighs a mere half an ounce.

They have the most rapid heartbeat of any avian, up to 1,260 times per minute—faster

▲ A fork-tailed wood nymph displays its shiny green throat and blue feathers as it lands. It breeds in Costa Rican rainforests, and favors heliconia flowers.

▶ It takes many calories to fuel a hummer like this young Allen's. Sometimes it doesn't get enough food or rest. To save energy, this bird goes into a special state of rest called torpor, which slows down the bird's heartrate and breathing. Torpor also helps hummers survive cold nights.

than any mammal except the shrew. They have the largest heart to body size as well.

Are you ready for more superlatives? Hummingbirds possess the fewest feathers—and the thickest plumage. Their tiny brains, 4.2% of body weight, are proportionately the largest in the bird kingdom. But it's their energy output, the highest of any warm-blooded animal, that impresses us most.

As they hover, they use, relative to size, ten times the energy of a 170-pound man running nine miles per hour. Try to imagine that same man, wanting to live the life of a hummingbird. To do so, he would need to consume more than 150,000 calories a day.

As they fly, forage, and fight, hummers burn fuel faster than a race car. If a bird doesn't get enough to eat by sundown, or the weather is cold, it uses a strategy called torpor. Fluffing out its feathers, the bird slows its heartrate, and lowers its body temperature so it can survive until morning. Although some rodents, reptiles, and bats do this, hummers are the only birds that can go into torpor.

Mountain meadows in bloom are favorite feeding places for many U.S. species, including the rufous, the black-chinned, the broad-tailed, and the calliope hummer, the smallest bird in North America.

From wingtip to warble

*T*iny yet incredibly complex, the hummingbird can go from zero to full speed from its perch, move instantly in any direction, and land without slowing down. It can even fly short distances upside down, a trick it uses when being attacked by another bird. The only aerial feat a hummingbird cannot do? Soar with its wings held still.

The way a hummer's wings are put together involves more firsts. It's the most helicopter-like of all birds. Up to 30% of the bird's weight consists of flight muscles. The shoulder joint resembles a ball and socket, letting the wing rotate 180 degrees. With most bird species, the up-stroke of the wing simply returns it to its place. In the hummingbird, it adds propulsion and

▶ A male Anna's hummer plunges his bill into a red gladiolus flower. Many plants sport red flowers to attract these busy birds with the lightning-fast tongues.

lift. To hover, hummingbirds move their wings forward and backward in a repeated figure eight. Up-stroke and down-stroke match, pinning the bird in place, as if it were treading water. The tail helps steer, serving as rudder and brake. When flying slowly, the hummer often spreads its tail feathers, which gives it extra lift.

As a rule, the smaller the bird, the faster the wing. Hummingbirds have the fastest wingbeats of any class of birds. They aren't the fastest flyers, however. They move at roughly the same speed as songbirds and pigeons. Their quick, zippy movements and small size give us the illusion of greater speed.

To learn more about how fast hummers fly, scientists have carried out wind tunnel experiments. In their tests, ruby-throated hummingbirds reached 30 miles per hour.

▲ Built for power and dazzle, hummingbirds are mostly flight muscles covered with flashy feathers. Their tails are used for flight, for quick stops, and for display.

Other field observations have shown that the ruby-throated can do 50 miles per hour when it needs to get away from a rival—and a fierce 63 miles per hour when showing off for a female in a courtship dive.

Both the Anna's and the Allen's hummingbirds have been timed doing 60 mph in courtship dives. But the champion speedster has to be the lovely green violet-ear hummingbird, once documented at a blistering 90 miles per hour during a short chase.

As far as wingbeat speed: ruby-throateds beat their wings a modest 53 times a second, but pour it on in courtship dives. Ruby-throated and rufous hummingbirds accelerate to 200 beats per second during their dives. That speed gives the rufous a special whistle to its wing zinging.

Hummers usually wear ten tailfeathers; but species in the tropics often have long showy tails. Some tails even make noises, and boast neon-bright colors that wink on and off. Tropical males may also wear fancy crests on their heads, to impress potential mates.

A hummer is so excellent at acrobatic flying that most species barely walk. They manage minor hops, but use wings to move down a twig or shift themselves on the nest.

▼ An Allen's hummingbird returns to her chicks in the nest. Sometimes before feeding them, she wiggles her long pale tongue.

Bills and tongues are as specialized as wings. Scientists believe that hummingbirds originally visited tropical flowers to hunt insects. Little by little, they wound up powering themselves on nectar, and their bills became longer and more slender. Plants evolved too, modifying flower shapes to attract more hummers. Today, birds and flowers have adapted so well to each other that a hummer's bill can slip into the corolla of its favorite flower as easily as a sword slides into a scabbard.

Inside the bill is a long pale tongue that darts deep into the flower for nectar, quicker than your eyes can see. The hummer's tongue sucks up liquid through capillary

▼ Hummers require protein in their diet as well. They catch spiders, pick bugs off twigs, and snap gnats from the air.

► In their nonstop quest for flight fuel, hummingbirds visit more than 1,000 flowers a day, like these foxgloves. They need long bills and longer tongues to get deep into tube-shaped blossoms, where the sweet nectar is.

action, just the way a towel absorbs water. The brushy tip of the tongue also traps insects looking for nectar—and the hummer gets a bit of protein with its breakfast.

Bill shapes echo the shapes of nectar-rich flowers. They may look like pins, or swords, or curved like sickles. The bills of most hummingbirds curve downward; just two species have bills curving upward. The swordbill hummer has a bill as long as the rest of its body.

Plants that depend on hummingbirds to spread their powdery grains of pollen do all they can to please. Their blossoms open during daylight hours, when hummingbirds are most active. Flowers project outwards, so the bird won't get caught in foliage. Many have flowers shaped like trumpets. Often, the flowers lack a place to perch, letting hummers take in nectar while hovering, and discouraging competitors such as bees and butterflies, as well as non-pollinating insects. Since hummingbirds have no ability to smell, their feeding flowers do not need to be scented.

In the United States, many flowering plants compete for attention of the ruby-

throated, which feeds on the nectar of 31 different plant species in North America. In temperate zones like the United States, many flowers have similar shapes. Hummers that visit them have evolved bills that are straight or slightly curved to match. In the tropics, thousands of species of plants and birds compete for food and pollination in a small area. This encourages specialization of flower parts, and specialized bills to fit them.

Hummingbirds have better color vision than human beings, and find their flowery foods by sight. Besides the colors we see, they see in the ultraviolet spectrum, which is invisible to us. Red blossoms—a color invisible to bees—get their special attention. Some researchers believe that migrating hummingbirds search for flowering plants from the air. Bright red blossoms may be easier for them to spot. Reds and yellows do predominate among the flowers the hummingbird visits, particularly in the United States, where plants have hit upon common strategies.

Newly fledged chicks head for red blossoms, learning by trial and error which ones yield the most nectar. But they quickly learn to visit flowers of all kinds. Their focus is nectar, not color. In the tropics, ornithophilous or bird-loving plants are more apt to wear a variety of colors besides red.

Hummingbirds feed on insects too, both in the flower and in the air. Their menu items include aphids, ants, fruit flies, mites, mosquitoes, gnats, flies, and spiders. Since the sweetness of a flower's nectar also attracts insects, hummers can nibble while sipping. They also pull insects out of spiderwebs, including the spider itself.

To catch insects on the fly, hummers open their beaks and grab insects, one by one. When they hunt insects on plants, it's called gleaning. Most hummers do it while hovering. In the Andes Mountains, however, two unusual species of strong-legged hummingbirds walk on the ground while gleaning.

Insects provide needed protein, and tide birds through winters when there are no flowers at all. Insects also furnish important fuel for baby hummers to grow. The ratio of nectar to insects varies from species to species.

Holes made in tree trunks by birds called sapsuckers are a double treat for hummers, netting both insects and sweet sap. Some species, like the rufous, ruby-throated, Anna's, and broad-tailed hummingbirds, depend on sap, especially before flowers bloom in the spring, and while migrating.

Although a hummingbird's wings and bill are well-developed, the same can't be said for its voice. Most hummingbirds make lousy singers. The Allen's hummingbird is able to trill a few notes; the Costa's gives a pretty whistle at the end of its call; and the white-eared hummer makes a bell-like sound. The wine-throated hummer of Guatemala sings a minute-long song. Mexico's wedge-tailed sabrewing even bears the nickname nightingale hummingbird. But these species are the exceptions. Most hummingbirds can manage only chirps, squeaks, and twitters, although they deliver them with drama.

This is not to say that hummingbirds don't try to sing. Whenever they defend flowers or chase intruders, which is frequently, they keep up a nonstop chatter of tuneless screeches.

The noise made by the Anna's hummer has often been compared to the sound of a rusty nail in a tin can.

Hummers produce a variety of other noises by zinging, a sound produced by their wings, not their vocal chords. Each species has its own zing, rung by its own wingbeat from the vibrations of its long, narrow feathers.

The noisy, zinging hum of a ruby-throated, the best-known hummer in the United States, and the species first encountered by English-speaking settlers to North America, probably gave rise to the bird's common name of hummingbird. In other parts of the world, like Cuba, softer-voiced species got names like zum-zum.

Just when you think that the lives of hummers hold no more surprises, you stumble across them bathing. Much too independent to groom each other, these birds still need to keep their feathers flight-ready. To refresh themselves, they hover in the rain, near lawn sprinklers, in dripping foliage, and under waterfalls. They rub themselves on large wet surfaces, such as banana leaves. They sit in birdbaths and splash like finches. In the mountains of Baja California I have seen xantus hummingbirds gather below a one-inch waterfall until there were 11 of them lined up in a row. The sight of those tiny creatures all squeaking and splashing at once is as amusing a sight as I've seen in the natural world.

▲ The shy xantus, a Mexican species that ventures from time to time into Arizona and California, is an extremely uncommon sight. This is one of only a handful of photographs of this rare species.

One of the hummingbird's qualities that never fails to delight is its ability to broadcast color. As the bird moves, it becomes a rainbow. Its colors change, winking on and off. Its head and throat may flash magenta or purple, then fade to black. Its colors slide from copper to gold to green, right before your eyes. As the fiery little flyer turns toward the sun and away from it, you get a nonstop light-show.

The hummingbird's winking, neon-like color changes are called iridescence. A few creatures—peacocks, butterflies, beetles, and fishes—also sport iridescent colors. Partly due to the hummer's movement, its iridescent feathers seem more alive.

Most color that reaches our eyes is created by pigment. The iridescence of hummingbirds is called structural color. In the top layer of their feathers, there are structures: special cells. When light hits these cells, some of it is made more intense, and some of it disappears. This cell structure lets light go in a single direction, like a lighthouse beacon. Its effect can be seen from only a certain angle. The result is

▶ It takes hummingbird males a year to develop the gorgeous gorget or throat patch. Rainbow-bright hummer feathers are iridescent. They let male birds flash their colors or hide them, to impress females or threaten other males. Females have less biological need to advertise in color.

▲ On rare occasions, animals are born which lack all or most of their color. We call them albinos—from the Latin word for white. This hummingbird, sipping from a fuchsia flower, is a partial albino. Its feathers are white but it has black eyes.

color that shimmers and changes and jumps at you.

The most electric colors go onto the hummer's head and throat. Males wear the richest shades. In the United States, hummingbird iridescence may range from red to purple. Further south, hummers flaunt a rainbow of colors from pale gold to deepest blue. A great many species also have feathers of metallic green on their backs, iridescent but less brilliant.

Hummingbirds also have colors produced by regular pigmentation. Because they need to stay hidden while raising young, the feathers of most females tend to be pigmented with colors that don't stand out—white, gray, or brown—with touches of red or gold iridescence here and there. Some species, particularly the rainforest group of birds known as hermits, are as dull-colored as sparrows. But, for hummingbirds, drab is the exception.

▶ Hummers like this rainforest hermit get powdered with pollen from the flowers they visit, which often hides their markings. The male hummingbirds of most species wear much brighter colors than the drab browns and grays of the hermit.

Showy species often live in tropical rainforests, or in cooler cloud forests, like this one.

Some hummingbirds, like this red-tailed comet, wear bright head crests and long colorful tails. Others look just the opposite.

Defending the territory

Anyone who has watched hummers skirmish around feeders knows how aggressive these tiny beings can be. Most species have feeding territories which they defend from bees, other flower-loving insects, and other hummingbirds, male or female. Hummers also defend territories for breeding purposes.

Most feeding territories are held by males, but some by females and even by juvenile birds. Migratory species that defend larger patches of terrain tend to be more warlike than hummers living in more crowded tropical rainforests. In rainforests, groups of hummers tend to divide territory peacefully.

▶ Backyard brawls, like this one with ruby-throated hummingbirds fighting to drink at one feeder, can sometimes be avoided. Putting a second feeder in a garden, out of sight from the first, would be doing these tiny birds a great favor.

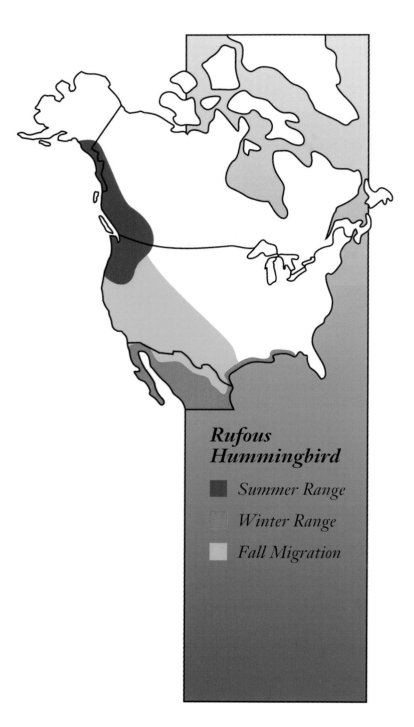

Rufous Hummingbird

■ *Summer Range*

□ *Winter Range*

■ *Fall Migration*

Hummingbirds have other ways of foraging, too. Medium-sized birds that take nectar from many types of flowers sometimes have a regular route they follow each day—rather than a territory.

To keep intruders from stealing their nectar supply, hummers get to work before sunrise, drinking from the flowers at the very edges of their territories. Even when not feeding, they will attack anything that ventures into their flowery terrain.

In defending their flowers—or their females—male hummers flash their colors angrily and dive at each other, claws and bill at the ready. They raise quite a ruckus. Most of the time they threaten without physical contact. Sometimes, however, two birds will tussle in flight and fall to the ground.

Hummingbirds seem to put up with each other only when there is more than enough food. Whenever these territorial warriors gather at a backyard feeder, the closeness brings out their worst—and most entertaining—qualities.

My own favorite fighter is the tiny rust-colored rufous, whose feathers turn into a cobweb of fire in the sun. He arrives at my feeder in the Rockies in late July, several weeks after the broad-tail hummers have laid claim to it. Sitting like a bulldog on a nearby twig, he sips at leisure and lunges at all comers, even when he isn't interested in feeding. He shows no mercy and is a most successful bird.

Most male and female hummingbirds come together solely to court and produce young. Each of the hummer species in North America has a unique courtship flight. The male does aerial acrobatics while the female hovers or sits and watches.

The male ruby-throated puts on quite a show. He plunges repeatedly back and forth in a U-shaped trajectory, regular as a pendulum, making a smacking noise at the top.

We see even more showmanship in the courtship dives of the male Anna's. Zooming 100 feet in the air, he plummets toward

▼ The wings of an Anna's are a blur, as it begins a courtship display. Besides singing a complex song, the male Anna's does aerial acrobatics, soaring and diving five or ten times in a row.

the female at 60 miles per hour, stops in front of her with an explosive booming of his tail, and hovers facing the sun to show his colors in full glory, madly squeaking all the while. Afterwards, he shoots straight up to repeat the maneuver.

A female judges a male hummer not only on his displays but on the number of flowers in his territory. Once she's been won over, she may join him in an aerial chase. Sometimes the two spiral through the air to her chosen nest site, in a courtship flight that's joyous to watch.

In the tropics where space to dive is limited, hummingbirds have developed quite a different system. Although the least impressive quality of any hummer is its voice, these males court by singing. They sing in groups, because their voices are so feeble that females would never find them otherwise. They gather in courtship assemblies called leks. From two to as many as 100 males, each on his own perch, sit together in a location that seldom changes over the years. It's a rare example of mutual tolerance.

The males repeat what may be a two-note squeak, over and over, while the females size them up. One species of hermit hummingbird sings its riff 12,000 times a day, every two seconds. Eventually, each visiting female makes her choice, rocketing away with her intended.

After these displays and vocalizations, hummingbird pairs speedily mate. They may spend a few minutes or as much as a day together. Few details are known about their mating habits, especially of those species that live in the rainforest.

▲ Female hummers do heroic work as single parents, making nests and raising chicks every year. Unlike other bird species, male hummers play no part in family life after courtship and mating. From then on, the female is on her own.

Hummers are unusual among birds because males play no part in rearing the chicks. Before choosing her mate, the female usually prepares the nest for her brood. She places it on twigs or logs, hides it among vines or cactus spines, or sticks it to the ceilings of caves or human dwellings. Some species prefer to be near a brook or running water. Spacing the nest well away from other females, yet close to food sources, is what the mother hummer is after.

Her walnut-sized nest can be finished in a day or fussed over for two weeks. She gathers all kinds of construction materials: plant fibers, seed husks, pine needles, shredded bark, cattail fluff, feathers, and wool. Thistledown, milkweed seeds, and the stems of young ferns soften the lining. Females stitch the walls of the nest together with spiderweb silk, glue them with saliva, and disguise them with lichen and mosses. Sometimes she braces the nest with mud, if the perch is precarious.

I once watched a Costa's hummingbird build a nest on a ficus twig three inches from a windowpane in Phoenix. The bird hovered over the nest and stabbed new material in with her bill. Sitting on the cup, she craned backward and tapped each addition into place. Then she rotated around the nest with a whirring of wings, shaping the exterior with the underside of her bill like an experienced potter.

Satisfied at last, she settled on the nest like the lid on a dollhouse teakettle.

A clutch of two white eggs is laid one or two days apart. Smaller than jellybeans, the eggs are the most minute in the bird kingdom. The female broods or keeps the

▼ Some hummingbirds are small enough to be mistaken for moths that also sip nectar. These eggs were laid by an Anna's hummingbird. Eggs from the Cuban bee, the world's smallest bird, are even tinier.

▲ Ingenious mothers use spider silk and saliva to hold their nests together. These Anna's babies, already growing pinfeathers but still blind, are under five days old. Bits of their shells still remain in this cozy, well-made nest.

eggs warm for 15 to 19 days. She leaves the nest only to feed and to fetch repair material, such as cobwebs.

Born blind, her newborns have naked black skin and look like raisins. The chicks never do grow any down, but immediately sprout pin feathers. As they wait for mama to bring insects, their bills protrude from the nest like a pair of sharp black needles. At first she feeds them every couple of minutes. Later she slacks off to three times an hour, plunging her bill deeply into their open mouths. After twelve days the chicks have enough feathers so that their mother can stop shading them from the heat of sun, or covering

► With her long sharp beak, a female pokes quantities of tiny insects, along with nectar, down the throats of her big chicks. Their feathers show they are close to the time they will fledge or fly away from the nest.

▼ By the time hummingbirds are ready to fly (at 25 or 30 days of age), they seem too big for their space, looking like two castaways about to sink a life raft.

them against a chill. With feathers comes the ability to regulate body temperature, an important step for baby hummers.

By the sixteenth day, hummer chicks begin to rehearse for flight, flexing their wings and rising slightly from the nest. Twenty-five to thirty days may seem like a long stay in the nest, but it's common for birds that must be able to fly on the first try. The fledglings leave with no prompting from their mother, sometimes managing to fly 50 feet on their first flight.

▲ After feeding, a mother hummer of the Anna's species shades her young from the sun. Until chicks are old enough to maintain their body temperature, mothers brood them to prevent over-heating or chilling.

The mother may still feed them and check up on them for a bit, but the youngsters soon mature and go their own ways. Mother has little time for extra parenting. Often she is building a nest for a second brood of chicks while still feeding the first. It's a system that works, as I learned when I watched a Costa's hummingbird successfully nest more than once in a loop of electrical wire in a carport, indifferent to the comings and goings of cars, dogs, and human beings.

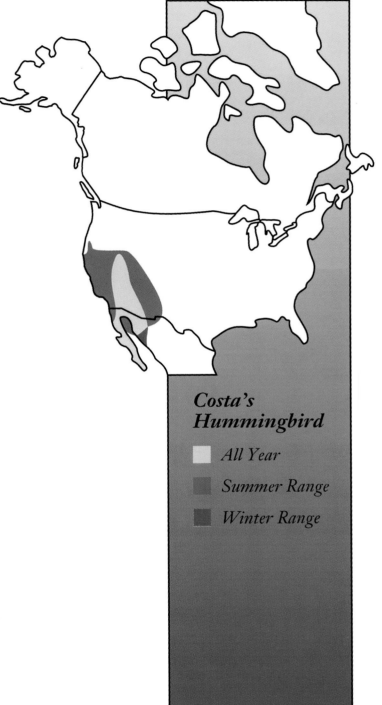

Costa's Hummingbird

All Year

Summer Range

Winter Range

Desert flowers in California, the southwestern United States, and Mexico present a feast to hummingbirds. Among the birds that return to the dry lands for these blooms are the buff-bellied hummer, the blue-throated (the largest U.S. species), and the Costa's (above), which wears purple on its head and throat.

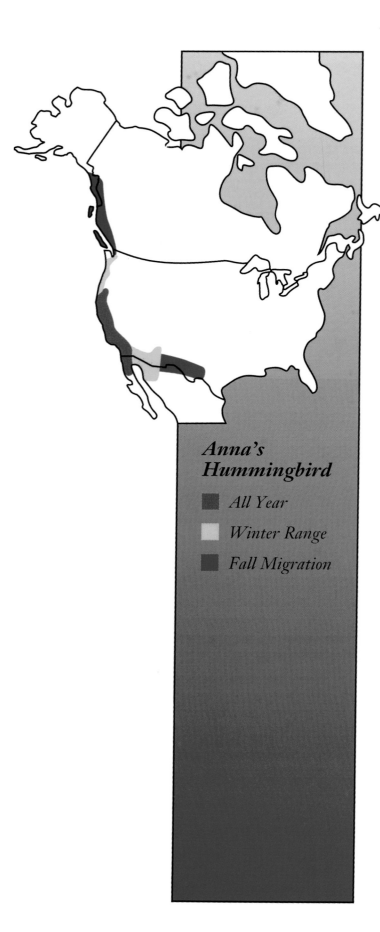

Anna's Hummingbird

- ■ All Year
- ■ Winter Range
- ■ Fall Migration

Hummingbirds in the wild may live two or three years, or as much as a decade or more. Females tend to outlive males. Not only do many hummers migrate long distances each year, they have prodigious memories. Anyone with a feeder can tell you that either the original birds or their offspring return from distant lands with unerring accuracy, year after year. (Site fidelity is what scientists call this ability of hummers to remember geography.)

A few years ago, I moved my feeder around a corner, thinking it might take them a day or so to relocate. The hummers found it in seven minutes, then checked the eaves to see if the house grew feeders the way an apple tree grows apples.

They must be smart as well as tough to maintain the dashing lives they lead. Species that migrate to the United States travel impressive distances. Many ruby-throateds make a 2,000-mile journey each spring from Panama to Ontario, Canada. The trip includes a 500-mile nonstop flight over the Gulf of Mexico. By flying more slowly to save fuel, and taking advantage of prevailing

winds, they can cross the Gulf on a gram of stored fat.

The rufous makes an even longer journey (over 2,200 miles each way) between the Mexican state of Guerrero and Alaska, where it ranges up to 11,000 feet. After breeding at the northern end of the circuit, this altitude-loving hummer returns south in a more leisurely fashion along the crest of the Rocky Mountains.

The Anna's hummingbird remains in the United States but migrates vertically. It breeds at low elevations during California's winter and spring, then heads for the flowery meadows of the Sierra Nevada Mountains for the summer.

To make their amazing migrations, hummingbirds bulk up beforehand. They power down insects and nectar to add extra body fat – up to 45% of their total weight.

Migration is instinctive behavior; males leave first, females second, and juveniles fly out weeks later. Migrating groups move from one remembered flowering area to the next—another feat of memory that amazes.

The energy demands on a hummingbird are huge: 12 times greater than the pigeon, 25 times greater than domestic chickens. To maintain themselves, hummingbirds must feed every ten to fifteen minutes, 50 or 60 times a day. Their life is a relentless buffet, beginning before dawn and ending after sunset. They consume up to five times their weight in food, and drink eight times their weight in water daily.

Being so small, hummingbirds lose body heat rapidly. They also lack insulating down feathers, which would cause them to overheat by day. To combat hunger, stress, and cold, at night they may sink into a torpor that brings their whole system nearly to a stop. Because nesting females need to keep their eggs warm, they don't go into torpor. But most other hummers do, on a regular basis.

For example, the Anna's hummingbird can drop its normal body temperature of 104 degrees to as low as 75. In torpor, the pulse of the blue-throated slows to a mere 36 beats per minute. Unlike normal sleep, this near-death state leaves the hummer more vulnerable to predators. In the morning, it takes the cold, stiff bird an hour or more to resume normal activities.

▲ In the Amazon rainforest, a quick snake makes short work of a hermit hummingbird.

Hummingbirds frequently chase crows, harass hawks, and pester bigger birds of all kinds. When they join forces with other small birds, hummers often lead the charge.

Being fearless and very fast, hummers have only a few serious enemies. Roadrunners, owls, and smaller hawks, like the kestrel, sometimes kill and eat them. In the rainforest, they can fall prey to praying mantises and snakes. On rare occasions, hummingbirds feeding at low flowers have been gulped by bullfrogs. There is also an astonishing eyewitness account of a hummer being downed by a leaping bass.

Hummingbirds regularly eat spiders. But on unlucky days, they may get entangled in webs and end up as the spiders' dinner.

As with other birds, hummingbirds are most vulnerable in their preflight days. Both chicks and eggs are preyed upon by cats, jays, ants, rodents, raptors, and snakes.

The exploding population of human beings on this planet represents the most serious threat to hummingbirds. With our numbers and our nonstop need to expand, change, and develop wild lands and waters, we are crowding out the wild creatures and birds that give our lives true meaning.

As with many other species we endanger, the greatest problem faced by hummingbirds is habitat loss, particularly forest and rainforest lands. The winter quarters for many migratory species are in jeopardy. Habitat destruction and degradation also evict tropical species from their permanent homes. Logging, mining, and road-building wipe out wildflowers and nectar sources, making it harder for these small birds to refuel while migrating.

In spite of the destruction that human beings have brought into their lives and territories, hummingbirds remain unafraid, curious, and confiding. In the wild, they let us observe them at work, at play, at mothering, at courtship. At feeders, they will sometimes land quite calmly on a finger that is substituted for a perch.

To assure a bright future for these brilliant birds, we need to preserve and protect their migratory paths. We need to keep their many and varied habitats intact. Most of all, we need to share the resources of nature with these sparkling creatures who do the all-important work of pollinating our plants and give us so much simple pleasure at the same time.

With luck, with work, and with continuing good will on our part, the zing and dazzle of hummingbirds will continue to gladden us—and future generations.

►This clever mother has neatly hidden her nest inside a metal chain. When her babies are tiny, she feeds them a lot of nectar. Later, their diet includes insects, producing a lot of waste matter. By instinct, baby hummingbirds know how to expel their wastes from the nest.

Secrets of hummingbirds

- Each day, hummers need to drink nectar from at least 1,000 flowers. Their long tongues sip nectar faster than your eye can see—about a dozen sips per second.

- It takes about 15 minutes for a hummer to digest a nectar meal.

- These small birds are sometimes mistaken for bees and other insects. At other times, nectar-loving insects like the hawk moth are mistaken for hummingbirds!

- Most males wear iridescent feathers on parts of their bodies. But only one-third of each feather—just the part that shows—is iridescent.

- World champions at flight, hummers can flap their wings up to 200 beats per second.

- When migrating, hummingbirds take it slower. But they still beat their wings up to 50 times per second.

- The courtship dive of a hummingbird can reach 60 miles per hour or more. See-through membranes, like swim goggles, protect their eyes.

- It always appears to be in motion, but a typical hummingbird spends more time perching than on any other activity.

- Hummingbirds are the only birds in the world that can lower their heart rate and temperature. This energy-saving state is called torpor.

Glossary

Avian. Referring to birds.

Brood. To sit on or hatch eggs. A female hummer also broods her chicks by warming, protecting, or covering them with her wings or body.

Clutch. A group of newly hatched eggs.

Corolla. Part of the flower or plant that holds the nectar.

Courtship displays. Dives, songs, and other activities performed by a male to persuade a female to mate with him.

Fledge. Able to fly. A fledgling is a young bird that has just taken its first flight, on its way to becoming an adult.

Gorget. Throat area of the hummingbird, often covered with colorful iridescent feathers. Male birds display gorgets to attract females and threaten other males. A few female species have iridescent feathers on the gorget also.

Indigenous people. The original human inhabitants of an area or country.

Iridescence. A type of coloration called structural color. Brighter than pigment, it winks on and off. Hummers often have iridescent throats, heads, backs, and tails.

Lek. Place where male hummingbirds assemble to display and sing, to attract females for mating.

Ornithophilous. Plants that have adapted, through flower colors or shapes, to attract birds, such as the hummingbird.

Preening. To groom or clean feathers or fur. Hummingbirds do not preen each other. Their spines are flexible enough so they can preen themselves.

Sapsucker. A group of birds that drills holes in tree trunks. Some hummingbirds, like the ruby-throated, also feed on sap from these holes.

Torpor. A state in which hummingbirds can lower their heartbeats and body temperature to save energy and survive chilly nights.

Trajectory. Path made through the air by a fighting or courting hummingbird.

Trochilidae. Scientific name for the hummingbird family

Zing, zinging. The sounds made by hummingbird wingbeats. Each species has a different sounding zing.

◄An Allen's hummingbird female can hover in place like a helicopter as she drinks nectar from a bottlebrush plant.

About the author
Bruce Berger lives in Colorado and Baja California. His other books on the natural world include *The Telling Distance,* winner of the Western Book Award, and *Almost an Island: Travels in Baja California.*

Photographers
Sixteen extraordinary photographers appear on these pages. The broad-billed hummingbird on the front cover is by Wayne Lankinen. The ruby-throated on the back cover is by Stephen Krasemann.

 John Chellman/Animals Animals, p. 18; Kay Comstock, p. 36; Michael Fogden/Animals Animals, p. 25; Clayton Fogle, pp 21, 28-29. 32, 33, 43, 46; Jeff Foott, pp 17, 38 inset; John Gerlach/DRK Photo, p. 19; Francois Gohier, pp 14-15, 16, 27 inset, 31, 35; Marcia Griffen/Animals Animals, p. 4; Richard R. Hansen, pp 10, 11, 24, 34, 37, 41; Noah Hawthorne, p. 42; Stephen Krasemann/DRK Photo, back cover;Wayne Lankinen/DRK Photo, front cover, pp 6-7, 9, 13; George Lepp/Comstock Inc, pp 1, 23; Pat O'Hara/DRK Photo, pp 12-13; L.L.T. Rhodes/Earth Scenes, pp 38-39; and Doug Wechsler/Earth Scenes, pp 26-27.

Special thanks
• Richard R.Hansen, wildlife photographer & biologist
• Julie Dahlen, Children's Librarian, Paso Robles Public Library
• Noah Hawthorne, science researcher at Tambopata Reserve, Peru
• Kelly Cash & Debbie Collazo at the Nature Conservancy
• Norma Lee Browning and Russell Ogg

Where to view hummingbirds
• Please remember the responsibilities that go along with the joy of watching and photographing hummers. Never interrupt activities, or disturb birds while nesting or foraging. Whether you watch them in the wilderness or your own backyard, respect and protect hummer habitats—don't pick flowers, remove brush, or remove blooms to get a better shot.

Because of space limitations, the following is a partial list.
United States:
• **Arizona:** in the southeast corner, the hummer-friendly

towns of Portal, Patagonia, Hereford, and Sierra Vista; in Tucson, the Arizona-Sonora Desert Museum and the U. Arizona campus; the Patagonia-Sonoita Creek Preserve; Nature Conservancy's Ramsey Canyon Preserve; Chiricahua National Monument; and Saguaro National Monument.
- **New Mexico**: Silver City; Gila Cliff Dwelling National Monument, near Silver City; Lake Roberts.
- **Texas**: Rockport, Lake Jackson, Fort Davis.
- California: Yosemite, Kings, and Sequoia National Parks; Anza-Borrego State Park; Kern River Preserve; the Channel Islands.

Outside the U.S:
- The cloud rainforests of Costa Rica; the hummer-rich islands of Jamaica, Puerto Rico, and Cuba; and rainforests in Mexico, Guatemala, Panama, Peru, and Brazil.

Events & Festivals:
- Hummer/Bird Celebration, Rockport TX
- Fort Davis Hummingbird Festival, Ft Davis TX
- Xtreme Hummingbird Xtravaganza, Lake Jackson TX
- Hummingbirds of New Mexico Festival, Lake Roberts NM
- Grey Feathers Hummingbird Festival, Silver City NM
- Hummingbird Fest, Land between Lake NRA, KY
- Hummer Celebration, Kern River Preserve, Weldon CA
- Hummingbird Migration Celebration, Holly Springs MS
- Festival of Hummingbirds, Tucson AZ
- Southwest Wings Birding Festival, Sierra Vista AZ
- Feliciana Hummingbird Celebration, St Francisville LA
- Folsom Hummingbird Festival, Folsom LA
- BirdFair and World BirdFest, both held annually in Britain

Helping organizations & good websites
- The Hummingbird Society (www.hummingbird.org) has an active membership of 2,500. Valuable quarterly, information-rich website; their mission is to educate and protect all hummer species. Sponsors of the annual Festival of Hummingbirds in Tucson, AZ.
- Through its website (www.nwf.org), the National Wildlife Federation sponsors eNature.com, a great guide to hummers in your local area. You can search by species, too.
- Earthwatch Institute, 3 Clock Tower Place, #100,

Maynard MA 01754. Web: www.earthwatch.org. Kids can become members, learn about important studies being carried out worldwide to save species and habitats from hummingbirds to rainforests. Ages 16 and up can take part in over 150 expeditions. Invaluable resource for educators.
- National Audubon Society, now partnered with BirdLife International for global coverage, has a tremendous range of programs, publications, and ways to help. The website (www.audubon.org) is outstanding, and local chapters are very active.
- Nature Conservancy plays a major role in land purchase for habitat preservation. Web: www.nature.org.
- Operation RubyThroat: the Hummingbird Project. The website (www.rubythroat.org) is interactive and focuses on one species.
- Globe program: (www.globe.gov). This fascinating hands-on science program in schools is worldwide. Through the internet, downloadable materials, and teacher training, Globe teaches kids how to conduct research field observations, enter data, and interact with real scientists. One of its programs focuses on the ruby-throated hummingbird.

To learn more
Books & Magazines
- *The World of the Hummingbird,* by Robert Burton (Firefly Books 2001). Big, superbly detailed book by a noted zoologist. The colorful photos rival the birds themselves.
- *Hummingbirds,* by Ben Sonder. (Courage Books 1999). Another well-written book with highest quality photos, plus a useful A to Z section on all North American species.
- *Hummingbirds, Their Life and Behavior,* by Esther & Robert Tyrell (Crown Books 1985). A classic; still valuable for its detailed fieldwork, amazing behavioral photos. Useful lists of species & of hummer-pollinated wildflowers.

Videos
- "Birds of the Sun God." BBC 1987. David Attenborough narrates this classic film.
- "Hooked on Hummingbirds." 55 minutes. Excellent new DVD, produced by Thomas Kaminski 2004.

Index